ME AND MY FEELINGS

ME and MY FEELINGS

A Kids' Guide to Understanding and Expressing Themselves

VANESSA GREEN ALLEN, MEd, NBCT

Illustrations by Sarah Rebar

ROCKRIDGE
PRESS

For general information on our other products and services or to obtain technical support, please contact our Customer Care Department within the U.S. at (866) 744-2665, or outside the U.S. at (510) 253-0500.

Rockridge Press publishes its books in a variety of electronic and print formats. Some content that appears in print may not be available in electronic books, and vice versa.

Interior and Cover Designer: Liz Cosgrove
Art Producer: Michael Hardgrove
Editor: Orli Zuravicky
Production Editor: Andrew Yackira
Author Photo: © Tarsha Burroughs
Illustrations: © 2019 Sarah Rebar; Shutterstock/mejnak, p. 19;
Shutterstock/VectorsMarket, p. 52.

ISBN: Print 978-1-64152-496-4   eBook 978-1-64152-497-1

To my daughter Domonique—
you are my *dream* come true!

CONTENTS

6. WHAT TO DO WHEN... 96

A LETTER TO GROWN-UPS

Dear Grown-Ups,

I am thrilled that you recognize the importance of kids understanding their emotions and feelings enough to provide the special child in your life with this book. My goal is to help kids feel empowered in knowing how to deal with their emotions and in learning healthy ways to express themselves.

By reading this book, kids will learn that all of their feelings are okay and perfectly natural to have. They will learn to separate their feelings from who they are as a person. Once they learn the best ways to deal with their negative emotions, they'll realize that they have the power to take control of their feelings and no longer be controlled by them.

This book explores many emotions and feelings. Many of the feelings we'll cover stem from the six big emotions I'll introduce in the first chapter. Although there's a lot of information packed into these pages, I also provide a variety of interactive activities that will allow kids to engage as they learn more about themselves, including:

- **Practices**, including visual tools and grounding techniques to use in different situations

- **Exercises**, in which kids can choose specific answers that apply to them, then learn what their responses mean

- **Quizzes** to help kids focus on what they are learning in the chapter

- **Express Yourself** tips that give kids helpful ways to express their emotions and feelings

- **Love Yourself** tips that help kids show self-compassion when dealing with their feelings and emotions

Thank you for sharing this book with the young reader in your life. I hope this book inspires learning, conversations, and actions that strengthen his or her emotional capabilities!

Yours truly,
Vanessa Allen

A LETTER TO KIDS

Dear Reader,

My name is Vanessa Allen and I am a school counselor in North Carolina. I help kids with their emotions and feelings at my school every day. It's a regular part of what I do, and it is very important. This is why I'm so happy that you are reading *Me and My Feelings* to learn more about *your* emotions and feelings! The more you learn about them, the more ready you will be to handle them in different situations.

You will learn about the six big emotions, along with lots of other emotions and feelings you may have. You'll find out why knowing yourself is so important. You'll learn all about the "voices" in your head that sometimes make you feel nervous, or tell you that everything is fine. I call them Eddie and Thelma, and we'll get to know them in this book. They can both sometimes be helpful, but you'll learn which one of them should really be in charge!

You'll find out how feelings affect your body. You'll also learn how your feelings affect different parts of your life, like your relationships and your time at school. But one of the most important things you'll discover in this book are awesome tips and suggestions to help you manage feelings when they seem too big to handle. By the time you finish reading this book, you'll know so many tips, you'll feel like you have a new superpower—and in a way, you will!

So what are you waiting for? Let's go earn your cape!

Yours truly,
Vanessa Allen

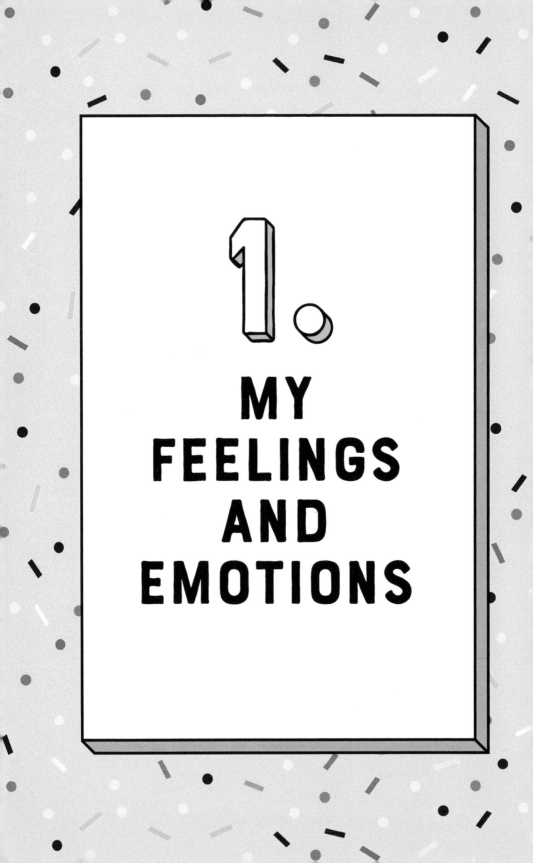

1.

MY
FEELINGS
AND
EMOTIONS

Have you ever noticed that some days you have a big smile on your face? You can't wait to hang out with your friends and do all your favorite things. Those days are pretty great, right? You've probably also noticed that some days you don't feel much like smiling at all. On those days, you may not want to play with your friends or even eat your favorite food. Those are the days you wish you could skip, right? Whether you are wearing a big smile and laughing, or choosing to spend some quiet time alone, you're feeling *something*. We all experience emotions and feelings every day of our lives—lots of them!

What's the difference between emotions and feelings, anyway? An emotion is how your body behaves when things happen to you. For instance, you may jump in surprise when someone pops out and says, "Boo!" A feeling can follow that emotion. You may feel angry because that "boo" made you spill your drink. Emotions and feelings play a big part in how your day goes. Think about it! Every day is full of new and different things that happen to you. These things give you all kinds of different feelings. Some feelings are good, and some are not

so good. It's totally normal for you to have all sorts of emotions and feelings from one day to the next, maybe even from one hour to the next! And guess what? You are not alone. Everyone you know has lots of emotions.

Your feelings can affect how you behave at home with your family, in school with your teachers and classmates, and when you're hanging out with your friends. Emotions and feelings are such a big part of life that it's important to understand them and where they come from. It's really helpful, too. Once you learn what you're feeling and why, you will know how to deal with it. You'll also be able to express, or share, those feelings with others in a healthy way, instead of just bottling them up inside you. I promise you, you'll feel a lot better once you do!

THE SIX BIG EMOTIONS

Let's talk about six of the biggest emotions that
everyone feels. These emotions can lead you to have
lots of different feelings, too.

Happiness: When you feel happy, you might smile or
laugh. You might even dance and sing your favorite
song. Happiness makes you feel good about things
in your life like school, your friends, and that test you
aced this morning.

Surprise: You might feel surprised when something
happens that you didn't expect. When you feel surprised, you might scrunch up your forehead. This is
because you're feeling unsure about what just happened. Your jaw might drop, or you might even jump
a little. Surprise can make you feel happy, but it can
also make you feel afraid or nervous. It all depends on
what the surprise is.

Fear: When you think you're in danger or feel like
something bad might happen, you experience fear.
If you see a big spider, you might feel afraid. Even
giving a report in front of the class can make you feel
this way. You may jump back and throw something
at the spider, or feel goosebumps or a stomachache
before class.

Sadness: When you feel sad, you might cry or want
to be by yourself. This feeling can happen if you

lose a pet or even a toy. You might also feel sad from being called names by someone at school or from not making the soccer team.

Anger: If you have ever felt like you were going to explode, you've probably experienced anger. Anger comes when something happens that you don't like. You might feel angry if somebody is being unfair, if you break a favorite toy, or if your mom says you can't sleep over at your friend's house.

Disgust: When you are disgusted, you might feel like you want to throw up. This emotion can happen when someone does something that's super gross. It can also happen when you see or smell something that stinks.

MORE EMOTIONS!

Okay, you're on a roll with the big six emotions—but there are so many more! Take a look at the emotions wheel below to see some other feelings and emotions that people feel all the time.

See how many emotions and feelings there are? And these are just a few! I bet you can find some on the wheel that you've had before—probably loads of times. You might feel nervous or shy when you meet someone new for the first time. You could feel embarrassed if you walk out of the bathroom with toilet paper on the bottom of your shoe. You might feel confused when a friend stops being nice to you, or a little jealous when your dog chooses to sleep in your little brother's room every night. The ways you can feel are endless. It is perfectly natural to feel all of these feelings. We all feel them. And this book is going to help you figure out what to do about them.

How Do I Feel?

Think about how you feel right now.

Now think about how you felt this morning. Do you feel the same way, or do you feel different somehow? Our feelings are always changing because new things are always happening. Circle all of the feelings that best describe how you've felt today and over the last couple of days.

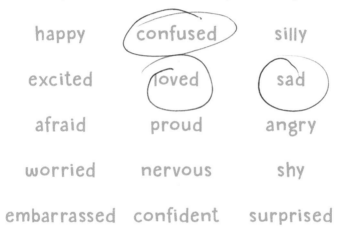

happy   (confused)   silly

excited   (loved)   (sad)

afraid   proud   angry

worried   nervous   shy

embarrassed   confident   surprised

Think about each word that you circled. Then use each one to complete this sentence:

I felt __loved__ when __Giovanni said happy b-day and text me!__

Did you learn anything? Did any of your answers surprise you? __wait yes. family makes me happy and loved.__

My Emotional Score

How well do you understand emotions? Don't be nervous! This isn't a test. Just read the statement, and then decide if that statement describes YOU never, sometimes, or often.

1. I can tell when a situation is making me upset by how my body feels.

   a. Never

   b. Sometimes

   c. Often

2. When I feel angry, I do something to calm myself down, like breathing or counting.

   a. Never

   b. Sometimes

   c. Often

3. I'm able to tell how other people are feeling by looking at their faces and what their bodies are doing.

   a. Never

   b. Sometimes

   c. Often

4. I help my friends with their own hard feelings by giving good advice and being a good example.

   a. Never

   b. Sometimes

    c. Often

Give yourself 1 point for every a, 2 points for every b, and 3 points for every c.

What's your score? _____

If your score was 4–5: It could really help to get to know your emotions a little better, and this book will show you how. Keep reading to learn more!

If your score was 6–10: You are pretty close to understanding your emotions. Keep reading to increase your score even more!

If your score was 11–12: You have a great understanding of your emotions. Keep reading this book to make it even better!

Yay!

EMOTIONS VS. MOODS

Now you know that there are lots of different emotions and endless ways to feel. I bet you have a pretty good idea which emotions make you feel good and which ones don't. Emotions and feelings can definitely put you in a *mood*. When we think of moods, we usually think of them as being either good or bad. You will be in a *good* mood if something awesome happens to you, or if many awesome things happen in a row. And good moods are great!

But when you get mad at your friend or have a problem you don't know how to fix, you just might find yourself in a *bad* mood. Sometimes we try to ignore our bad moods or just get over them without understanding them. But when you're in a bad mood, it's really important to take the time to understand why you're feeling that way. Once you figure out what's really wrong, you have a better chance of fixing the problem. And that will help you come out of your bad mood a LOT faster. Plus, you won't take your bad mood out on others. That's a win for everyone.

EXPRESS MYSELF!

No matter what is causing a bad mood, you can do a few things to make it better:

- Use your words to let others know when you're not in a good mood.

- Try not to take your bad mood out on others.

- Talk with someone you trust about what is bothering you.

- Cry if you need to.

- Give yourself some time alone until you feel better.

FEELING GREAT

Have you ever heard of the game, "Would You Rather"? Well, if you asked your friends, "Would you rather be happy or sad? Excited or angry? Relaxed or nervous?" I bet they would all agree: Happy, excited, and relaxed are the better choices. You would probably agree, too. Everyone likes feeling great! When you feel great, you do better in school, you get along better with others, and you are more likely to try new things. Here are some other good, or positive, feelings to learn about:

Hope: When you are hopeful, you expect good things to happen. This emotion is helpful even when things aren't going so well. When you're hopeful, you believe things can get better.

Joy: When you are joyful, you are really at your happiest. Joy is not an emotion that lasts for a long time. It comes around during the very best times, like when you get a new puppy or when you see someone you love after a long time apart.

Peace: When you are peaceful, your brain isn't full of worries. You are calm, which means that your mind is quiet and doesn't have a lot of stressful thoughts bouncing around inside it. Did you know that you can find ways to feel peaceful when things in your life aren't the best? Some of the exercises in this book can help you feel peaceful—try Seven Steps to Calm (page 88).

Positive emotions don't just make you happy—they also help you be the best YOU you can be. They make you feel great, and when negative emotions creep in, positive ones can help you get through them.

How Would I Feel?

When good things happen, you feel good, right? Let's see how you feel when different kinds of good things happen. Match the situations on the left with how you would most likely feel about them on the right.

While playing down the street from your house, you feel a few drops of rain. You make it into the house just before it starts to pour.

Your classmate has been talking about his big birthday party all week. Today, he gives you an invitation.

You're making funny faces at your sister and doing a dance to make her laugh, and it's working.

Taylor and Eric say you are a really good friend.

Your teacher tells your parent that you gave an awesome report in class on Monday.

It's Friday, and when you get home from school, you kick off your shoes and grab a blanket. You curl up on the sofa and begin watching your favorite show.

proud

silly

safe

relaxed

excited

happy

Do all of your answers match up to a situation? If so, great. You're in touch with your positive emotions. If not, that's okay, too—that's why you're reading this book!

FEELING NOT SO GREAT

Do you wish you could be happy all the time? I think we all do! The truth is, we won't always be happy. Sometimes we don't feel so great. No one likes to feel negative emotions. But did you know it's so much better to accept and deal with them than it is to avoid or ignore them? Here are a few common negative emotions and how they can make you feel. You may have felt some of these before, and that's perfectly okay.

Grief: This emotion happens when you lose someone close to you. It may be a person or a pet. When you are grieving, you are very sad. You may want to cry a lot and need lots of hugs and kind words from those who care about you.

Guilt: When you feel bad for something you did or didn't do, you feel guilty. Maybe you didn't tell your mom or dad the truth and your brother got into trouble instead of you. When you feel guilty, your stomach may feel upset or you may not feel like your usual self.

Disappointment: This emotion happens when something doesn't go the way you wanted it to. When you do your best but still don't pass your test, you may feel disappointed. You may also feel this way when you're not chosen for something, or when someone doesn't keep a promise. This emotion can make you feel sad and angry.

Believe it or not, good things can come out of negative emotions! They can make you notice things that are wrong and need to be changed or fixed. For example, if you feel guilty, you may need to admit you made a mistake about something.

They also help you stay safe in scary situations. Imagine if you saw a snake in your backyard. Fear might make you quickly run inside the house and close the door.

Finally, negative emotions can make you do things a different way so your next experience can be a good one. If you make a choice that upsets your mom or dad, you'll be more likely to think about it carefully the next time and make a better choice.

Climbing Out of the "Dumps"

Have you ever heard someone say they were "down in the dumps"? When a person is down in the dumps, they feel unhappy for some reason. There are days where you may feel angry, sad, or disappointed. When you are feeling down, you may think nonstop about what's making you feel that way, or you may not even know why you're feeling so down. Either way, you can do something to bring yourself back up—it's called the TV method.

Whenever you're watching TV and get tired of what's on, what do you do? You change the channel, right? So, why not try to change the channel in your mind? Switch off the "channel" in your mind that's making you feel bad. Instead, look for a new channel. Think about something that makes you smile. Focus on it. Draw it if you want.

It may take a little practice, but you can make a habit of "changing the channel." Once you can take control of those not-so-great emotions, you will get better at climbing out of the dumps!

LOVE MYSELF

When you're having a not-so-great day:

- Remember it's totally normal to have a not-so-great day. It happens to everyone.

- Give yourself permission to feel sad, angry, or afraid.

- Find ways to help yourself feel better, like writing about your feelings in a journal, or doing something kind for someone else. You might snuggle with your pet or make a special card for someone. And have hope— tomorrow will be better!

I CAN HANDLE IT!

A lot of people don't know how to handle their emotions and feelings—even some grown-ups. They focus on all the negative feelings and forget about the good ones. You are one step ahead of them because you have this book!

It's only been one chapter, but you've already learned:

- We all have many emotions, both positive and negative.

- There are six big emotions.

- There is a difference between emotions and moods.

- There are different happy emotions that mean different things.

- There are different not-so-great emotions with different meanings, but there are some helpful ways to handle them.

You're on a roll, but there's so much more! In the next chapters, you'll learn even more ideas to help you understand your feelings and helpful ways to get over bad feelings. You'll learn more about what makes you who you are, and how you can be your own best friend when things aren't going so great. You'll learn how to spot the things that make you upset, so you can either try to stay away from them or learn how to deal with them in a new and better way. You'll learn ways to calm down when you are worried or angry. Learning all of these things will help you stay in control of your emotions.

Your emotions and feelings are natural, but it can sometimes feel like there are just too many of them. Everyone feels that way sometimes. But once you start using all the skills you're about to learn, no matter what comes your way, you'll be able to say, "I can handle it!"

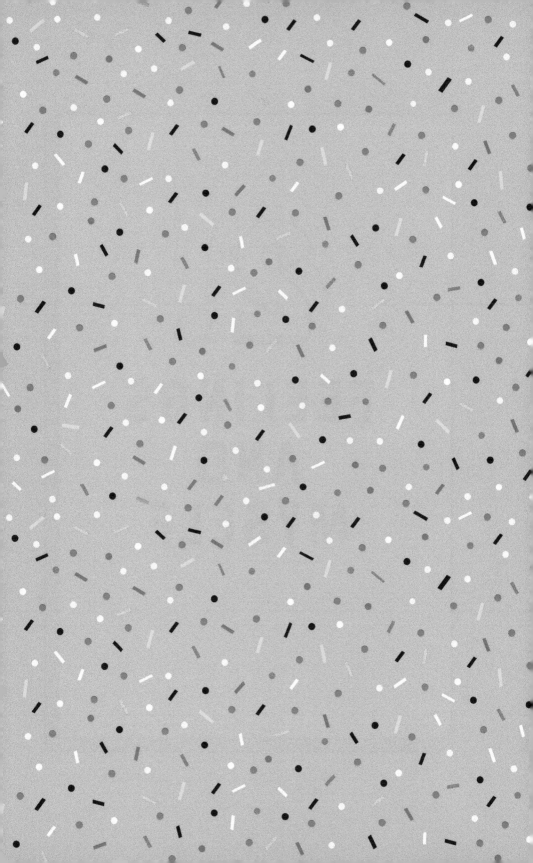

2.

FEELINGS
AND
MYSELF

In this chapter, we are going to get to know YOU! All the things you experience in your life create the puzzle that is you. The more you learn about yourself, the more you will understand your emotions and feelings. You'll be able to notice the things that scare you or make you angry. You'll also notice what things make you happy or excited. I'm sure you can think of some of these things in your mind already.

There are a lot of reasons why an experience might give you good or not-so-good feelings. Sometimes we know the reasons right away. For example, if you had a bad experience with a dog when you were younger, you may still feel scared whenever you are near dogs. You could be across the street from the friendliest dog in the neighborhood, but you won't want to go near it.

Other times, we don't know why we feel the way we do. When you learn about the things that cause you to have strong feelings, you won't be confused when they happen. There are even things you can do to change some feelings and how you react to them. But it all starts with getting to know yourself. Are you ready? Let's get to know YOU!

KNOWING MYSELF: HOW IT CAN HELP

If someone said, "Tell me about yourself," what would you say? You might tell them what food you love most, your favorite sport, or your favorite show. But there is so much more to you than just your favorite things! Knowing yourself also means paying attention to your feelings. When you know yourself, you can tell someone what makes you happy or angry. You also know what things you can use a little help with and what things you are a pro at.

You can also notice how your actions affect others. Knowing yourself will help you respond in the best way when things happen. It will also help you speak up for yourself when you need to. Here are a few examples of putting your feelings into action:

- Trey knew he was good at shooting free throws. When he found out that Gia was struggling to make her shot, he offered to help her.

- Ashley was talking to her friend during the movie. She noticed people turning around and looking at her. She stopped talking so they could hear the movie.

- Ricardo raised his hand to answer questions during math, and he felt upset when his teacher didn't call on him. On the way to lunch, he told his teacher that he wished she would call on him more.

When you really know yourself, you will feel more in control. That's because you are! You will notice the feelings you are having. You will also know exactly why you are having them. All of this can help you make positive changes to your own behavior.

I'M NOT MY FEELINGS

The fact that you feel many different things means your feelings are separate from who *you* are. It might be hard to see this at first, but changing the way you talk about your feelings can help. For example, if somebody makes you angry, instead of saying, "I'm angry," say, "I'm *feeling* angry." Because you are not an angry person—you just feel angry at the time. Remember: Feelings come and go. They don't make you who you are, and you have the power to control what you do with them. You can tell your angry feelings to calm down. You can also tell your nervous feelings that you will be okay.

When you don't use your power, your feelings can start to control you. What will happen then? Well, if your feelings take control, you might say things you wish you hadn't said, or do things you wish you hadn't done. You may not take a chance to try something new because you are afraid you won't be able to do it.

It's also important to realize that feelings don't always come one at a time. Sometimes you can have lots of different emotions and feelings all at once, and that's natural, too. When you remember that you are not your feelings, you'll begin to use your power no matter what emotions come knocking at your door.

Finding the Good Stuff

It's important to recognize "the good stuff" about you. Let's think about your character traits. Character traits are things about you that tell people the kind of person you are. Below is a list of positive traits. Think about what each trait means. Which ones describe you? Go ahead and circle your traits.

patient	helpful	kind
respectful	honest	dependable
responsible	brave	creative
loyal	polite	supportive
generous	loving	cheerful
thoughtful	caring	friendly

Although your feelings come and go, these positive character traits that you've chosen to describe you do not. They are here to stay! When your emotions make you feel down in the dumps, look back at your list of traits to remind yourself of all the positive things that make you who you are!

MIXED EMOTIONS

When I was a kid, my childhood friend and I both tried out for the cheerleading squad at our school. When the new team was posted, only I had made the squad. I was so excited that I was going to be a cheerleader. I was also very disappointed because my friend did not make the team. It's possible to have both good and not-so-good emotions at the same time, just like I did—it's called having mixed emotions. This is more proof that you are not your feelings. Imagine these situations:

* Jeremy was so happy to get the lead role in the school play. He also felt very nervous about performing in front of so many people.

* Renée was excited to learn to ride her new bike. She also felt angry and frustrated after she fell three times.

* Colby was happy his friend Juan could come to his birthday party, but he was sad that Juan couldn't stay for the sleepover.

It's perfectly natural to feel both good and not-so-good emotions at the same time. When this happens to you, pay attention to all your feelings. Think about how you can handle the negative feeling in a healthy way. Even though the negative feeling might really be bothering you, try your best to focus on the good.

LOVE MYSELF

Sometimes we feel bad about things. But even in hard times, it's possible to find the good in the bad with these tips:

- Believe in yourself, even when things go wrong. Try to think about what went right and celebrate that instead.

- If something you really want doesn't happen, take some time to think about what you do have, and be grateful.

WHAT MAKES ME ANGRY AND SAD

When anger or sadness come to my door, I do NOT want to let them in! Those two feelings just don't feel good. But the truth is, as hard as we may try, we can't keep them out. Just like we have our good times, there will be times that aren't so good. But you can remember that these feelings are just visiting for a little while—they won't stick around forever.

Sadness can happen for a bunch of different reasons. You will probably feel sad if you experience a loss, a huge disappointment, or if someone says or does mean things to you. When you feel sad, you might start crying. Crying is completely natural, and it helps soothe the pain you are feeling. A good cry can actually make you feel better sometimes!

Anger can be a response to many different situations. It all depends on the person. That's why it's important to know your anger "triggers." A trigger is something that causes you to become angry. Everyone's triggers are different. Maybe your triggers are kids who don't play fair, or not getting what you want. Even being hungry can make someone angry. (Have you ever heard the word "hangry"? It's really a thing!)

As you learn more about yourself, you can begin to learn *your* anger triggers. This is super useful. Once you know them, you can do your best to avoid them or learn how to not react impulsively when they happen. What does this mean? Well, when you react impulsively to your anger, you act without thinking first. You don't think about the consequences, or what might happen *because* of your actions. If you lash out and yell at your friend when he upsets you, you might say things you don't mean. Usually, impulsive behavior causes a bad ending. To avoid this, you can learn how to use self-control to respond in a different way. For example, if your first thought is to yell or scream, try to come up with a healthier way to express yourself. Maybe practice an action or line that you can use when it happens, like walking away or saying, "I want to play with you, but only if you play fair." Self-control will help you keep your cool on the outside even when you don't feel so cool on the inside.

EXPRESS MYSELF

When it comes to triggers and impulses, remember to:

- Pay attention to your body's response. Do your hands clench? Do your shoulders tense up? When you know your body's response to triggers, you'll know when it's time to control your actions.

- Remember: Stop-Breathe-Think! Take a moment to think about your response before you say or do anything.

Getting to Know Myself

Let's get to know more about who you are. Choose the answers that best describe you.

1. One word that describes me is:

    a. serious

    b. organized

    c. creative

    d. determined

2. My parents would say:

    a. I'm like a mini adult.

    b. I worry about things a lot.

    c. I have a great imagination.

    d. I like to win.

3. I often:

    a. think about how I will react to things.

    b. take a little longer to do things.

    c. get asked to stop talking in class.

    d. like to be the leader of my group.

4. When it's time for recess:

    a. I might be alone doing something I want to do.

    b. I'm fine just sitting and watching everyone else.

    c. I play with anyone who's having the most fun that day.

    d. I'm usually the best team captain!

If you chose mostly a's: **You are focused! You like to figure things out on your own. You like things a certain way, and you care about how others feel.**

If you chose mostly b's: **You are easygoing! You are calm most of the time. You don't like when there is conflict. You like when things are just right.**

If you chose mostly c's: **You are lively! You like to have fun. You are playful and like to make others laugh. You love to be around people.**

If you chose mostly d's: **You are adventurous! You enjoy being in charge. You like to make things happen.**

If you chose a mix of a, b, c, and/or d: **That's totally fine! Many people have qualities from more than one personality type. That just makes you extraordinary— and we knew that already!**

STRENGTHS AND WEAKNESSES: THEY'RE BOTH OKAY!

Can you name three things that you do well? How about three things that are hard for you? If you can't think of any right now, don't worry! As you get to know more about yourself, these are some of the things you'll learn.

The things you do well are called your strengths. You're usually able to do these things easily. You might be good at a certain subject, making friends, coming up with creative ideas, playing sports or an instrument, drawing, or something else. When you're good at something, you're confident when you do it.

The things that are harder for you to do are called your weaknesses. You may discover that reading is harder for you than it is for your best friend, or that you have trouble sharing your thoughts and feelings with other people. We all have weaknesses, and that's okay! But sometimes, when things are hard for us, we will feel negative emotions when we do those things. We may become worried, fearful, or angry. When this happens to you, just remind yourself that it's perfectly natural to have weaknesses, and that to get better at something, you just have to work a little harder!

Whether it's a strength or a weakness, all the parts of you are what make you who you are. Everyone has

strengths and weaknesses. Try not to compare yourself to someone else. Focus on *your* strengths, and
see your weaknesses as a challenge to be met. Don't
avoid the tough things—just know they're going to
take a little more time and energy, and you can do it!

My Strengths and Weaknesses

No one is perfect. We all have things we do well and things that aren't as easy for us. Below are several traits and skills. Circle your strengths. Underline your weaknesses.

organization

thinking positively

listening to others

being on time

making people laugh

being responsible

feeling confident

making friends

being creative

reading

math

writing

playing sports

eating healthy

speaking in public

being
patient

using
technology

completing
homework

being
a leader

using
self-control

playing
music

never
giving up

fixing
things

working
with others

staying
focused

telling
the truth

arts
and crafts

Are you surprised by any of your choices? I hope
you learned something interesting about yourself—
you are truly unique!

Self-Confidence Meter

Self-confidence is when you feel good about who you are and what you are able to do. Here's a self-confidence meter you can picture in your mind. The meter can help you decide how confident you are in different situations.

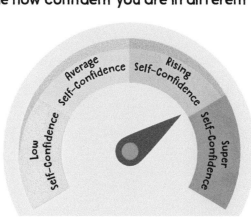

Your confidence will depend on the situation you are in. You may have "super self-confidence" when you play basketball, but you may have "low self-confidence" when you take a test at school. You can change this! When your confidence feels low, try to see yourself in your mind as the strong, confident person you *want* to be. Imagine yourself as a superhero saving the day. You can even think back to a time when you were successful. Use those feelings to give yourself a boost. And remember the saying, "Practice makes perfect." Continue to practice those things you want to build into strengths—this will help you become a more confident person!

I AM UNIQUE!

In this chapter, you learned:

- Some feelings are easy to understand; others are not, and we can feel more than one emotion at the same time.

- Our feelings are separate from who we are—they are always changing.

- Our traits are a part of us—they don't change.

- There are ways to handle sadness, and crying can be helpful.

- There are ways to identify your anger "triggers" and react in a calmer way.

- You have different strengths and weaknesses and there are ways you can build confidence.

Now that you know how to appreciate all the unique things about you, it's time to talk about how your feelings connect to your thoughts. Ready?

3.

FEELINGS
AND
MY MIND

Did you know your feelings make you think? When you feel a certain way, your brain starts working to figure out the reason. No matter what time of day it is, you are always thinking. Your thoughts help you deal with your feelings. And they are completely private. But guess what? Our thoughts don't always tell the truth! You may sometimes think something is true without knowing if it really is. For example, you may feel unhappy when you're at school. You might think your teacher doesn't like you. Or you may be worried that someone you care about will get sick. It's very possible that your thoughts in this situation are not true or realistic. This chapter will help you learn how to understand your thoughts so you can decide which ones are true and which ones are not. This will help you take control of any negative feelings. Let's get started!

Is My Mind Playing Tricks?

Below are some common thoughts people have all the time. Even adults have these thoughts sometimes! Check off the thoughts you've had.

_____ No one wants to be my friend.

_____ No one wants to hear what I have to say.

_____ Everyone thinks I'm dumb.

_____ I never do anything right.

_____ She's talking about me.

_____ No one wants to hang out with me.

_____ I'm not good enough.

_____ I am ugly.

_____ Something bad will happen.

    Now think about each of these thoughts and decide if they are really true or not. Could your thoughts or imagination be telling you these things? Chances are, your mind is accepting your negative feelings and turning them into negative thoughts that aren't really true!

MY TWO BRAINS: MY EMOTIONAL BRAIN AND MY THINKING BRAIN

Two brains?! You're probably thinking, "I don't really have TWO brains!" Let me explain. When it comes to your emotions and feelings, your brain has two personalities. These personalities are like roommates who "live" inside your head. Your emotional brain— we'll call him "Emotional" Eddie—is *always* on the lookout for danger. When Eddie sees a problem, he immediately wants to protect you, even if that means having you scream, "That's not fair!" when Dad says no more cookies.

Don't get me wrong. You actually need Eddie. Emotional Eddie will work to keep you away from danger. He might alert you that a car is speeding by so you don't step into the road. But his idea of danger may also be your classmate, Susan, cutting in front of you in line. He might tell you to push her out of the way because HEY, you were there first! Maybe not the best reaction, right?

And then you have your thinking brain. We'll call her "Thinking" Thelma. Thelma helps you think about situations before you act. She reminds you to use your self-control and to respond in the best way. When Susan cuts in line, Eddie might yell, "HEY! I was here first!" and encourage you to push Susan out of the way. But Thinking Thelma will jump in to remind you that pushing Susan will get you in trouble. Thelma will also remind you that instead of pushing Susan, you can calmly ask her not to get in front of you.

Emotional Eddie and Thinking Thelma can help you best when they work together as a team. But Thelma has to be stronger than Eddie. Watch out! Eddie will really want to take over when you feel embarrassed, nervous, or scared. Keep reading to learn how to help Thelma keep Eddie under control.

FEELING EMBARRASSED

Who likes to be embarrassed? No one *I* know! It can make you want to run and hide. I once sat on a table in the back of a classroom and accidentally made it tip over. I tipped over with it and all the stuff on it—*awkward*!

Different things might make you feel embarrassed. Maybe you tripped in the hall at school. You may have spilled your juice on someone else. And have you ever slipped up and called your teacher, "Mom?" Believe me, everyone feels embarrassed sometimes. Kids aren't the only ones—adults get embarrassed, too.

If you are embarrassed for doing something wrong, you might also feel ashamed. Feeling embarrassed may make your heart beat faster or make you start to sweat. You can thank Emotional Eddie for that! But if you listen to Thinking Thelma, you can find a way to face the embarrassment and then move on. If you don't make a big deal about it, the people around you will quickly move on, too. If it's funny, laugh it off. If it's awkward, say, "Well, THAT was awkward!" If you've done something wrong, apologize and try not to do it again. Turn your embarrassing moment into a time to show your courage and sense of humor.

Do My Emotions Rule Me?

Let's find out who's in charge—Thelma or Eddie!

1. When I have a hard day at school, I usually:

   a. take it out on others.

   b. take a little time out for myself.

   c. talk about it with someone.

2. When someone does something that upsets me, I usually:

   a. don't say anything at all.

   b. tell another person I'm upset.

   c. tell the person what he did that bothered me.

3. When I see something really sad, I usually:

   a. avoid it, even if I have to walk away.

   b. hold back my tears even though I feel them.

   c. let the tears flow.

4. When I am embarrassed, I usually:

   a. act like nothing ever happened, but then I think about it for days afterward.

   b. look around to see who saw what happened.

   c. make a joke about what just happened.

Give yourself 1 point for every a, 2 points for every b, and 3 points for every c.

What's your score? _____

If your score was 4–5: You usually keep your emotions to yourself. It can be helpful to express yourself in healthy ways. It's important to let it out, and let others know how you feel. Reading this book is the first step—you'll get there!

If your score was 6–10: You're on your way to taking charge of your emotions! You know what to do to feel better in some situations. In others, you may be less confident. Just keep trying, and you'll get there!

If your score was 11–12: Great job! You are not ruled by your emotions—keep doing what you're doing!

SOMETIMES I FEEL NERVOUS

One of the things I love to do is sing. I have performed by myself in front of hundreds of people. Even though I've been doing it for years, I *always* feel nervous when I grab the microphone. My heart beats a little faster, and sometimes my hands even shake.

These are just a couple of things that can happen when you are feeling nervous. Like all other feelings, being nervous is completely natural. It happens to everyone, and it can happen for many different reasons. You may feel nervous about a big test or about making good grades. You may feel nervous on the first day of school. You may also feel nervous when someone you care about is having a hard time. When you feel nervous, Emotional Eddie may cause you to feel stressed or even out of control. He's only trying to protect you, but it can be too much.

If you listen closely to Thinking Thelma, you'll feel braver and more in control. Thelma is telling you that there is no danger. To relax, try squeezing a stress ball or a fidget toy like putty or a cube, to keep your hands busy. If you are having a hard time catching your breath, imagine Thelma telling you, "It's okay. Take a few deep breaths—in through your nose, and out through your mouth. You've got this!"

How Nervous Would I Be?

Would any of these situations make you nervous? Rate each one on a scale from 1 to 5, with 1 being the least nervous and 5 being the most nervous, by circling the number that best represents how you would feel.

1 2 3 4 5 You have to sing a short solo during the chorus performance.

1 2 3 4 5 Your family moves and you're going to a new school after the holidays.

1 2 3 4 5 During a field trip, a lady brings out a snake for your class to touch.

1 2 3 4 5 You're about to ride a roller coaster that goes upside down.

1 2 3 4 5 You are chosen to introduce the mayor at the school assembly.

1 2 3 4 5 A news reporter in your neighborhood wants to interview you about the snow day.

Did you learn anything about yourself? What makes one person nervous might not bother another person at all. Have a friend rate each of these, too, and compare your answers!

EXPRESS MYSELF

When nervous feelings come your way, try to:

- Close your eyes and imagine being in a place that makes you feel calm and relaxed, like the lazy river at a water park.

- Find something to do to take your mind off what's making you feel nervous, like reading your favorite book or playing a fun game.

FACING FEARS AND WORRY: USING MY THINKING BRAIN

Think about something that you're afraid of. For me, it's mice! Now, do you have your fear in your mind? How does it make you feel in your body when you think of it? When I think of mice, my skin crawls. If I ever saw one in a room, I would probably jump on top of any chair, table, or desk I could reach. When that happens, it means Emotional Eddie has taken over!

Being afraid is natural. Some people may say, "I'm not afraid of anything." But *everyone* is afraid of something. Many kids are afraid of getting in trouble at home or school. Some are afraid of the dark. This might be triggered when there's a strong storm and the power goes out. When you're afraid, Emotional Eddie makes your heart beat faster. You may even breathe faster.

Worry is kind of like fear, except it sticks around in your head and causes you to think about it too much! You might be *afraid* of going to the dentist even when you don't have an appointment, but you might spend time *worrying* about your appointment when it's coming up next week.

The good thing is, feeling afraid or worried doesn't have to last. You can use your thinking brain to focus on something else to take your mind away from your concerns. If you turn to Thinking Thelma, you can go from thinking about the worst that could happen to thinking about what's more likely to happen, and how things will usually turn out fine. Changing your thinking can make you feel much calmer.

5-4-3-2-1

Remember, Thinking Thelma needs to be stronger than Emotional Eddie. Strengthen her with a good workout. Move those fearful thoughts to the side by focusing on your breathing and your senses in 5 . . . 4 . . . 3 . . . 2 . . . 1!

Breathe in through your nose for a count of three. Breathe out through your mouth for a count of five.

Think of five things that you can see.

Think of four things you can hear.

Think of three things you can feel.

Think of two things you can smell.

Think of one thing you can taste.

Finally, breathe in through your nose for a count of three. Breathe out through your mouth for a count of five.

I'm sure Thelma feels much stronger after that, and I hope you feel stronger, too! This simple breathing exercise takes the focus off nervousness and puts it on relaxation. That gives Eddie a break, and helps Thelma get stronger.

LOVE MYSELF

Are you having negative thoughts that you know deep down are not true? Be kind to yourself and try to:

* Be a friend to yourself! Think about what you would tell a friend if they were feeling what you feel, and use that to encourage yourself.

* Say something positive about yourself out loud—this really *can* give you a boost. Visit your list of positive character traits from the last chapter (page 41) whenever you need them!

I CAN OVERCOME NEGATIVE FEELINGS

Now that you know how your thoughts and feelings are connected, you are on your way to taking your power back. You've learned:

* Feeling nervous, embarrassed, and scared is natural.

- Different things make people nervous, embarrassed, worried, and scared—and *everybody* is scared of something, even if they don't admit it!

- Negative emotions will wake up Emotional Eddie. He will do whatever it takes to protect you, and sometimes he might go overboard.

- You can call on Thinking Thelma to calm things down. Your thoughts are powerful, but they are NOT the boss of you!

- You can say positive things to yourself to make you feel braver and stronger.

- Breathing can make Thinking Thelma stronger—and you more calm!

Now let's learn about what happens inside your body when your emotions are high. After all, you've got more exciting things to do than worry!

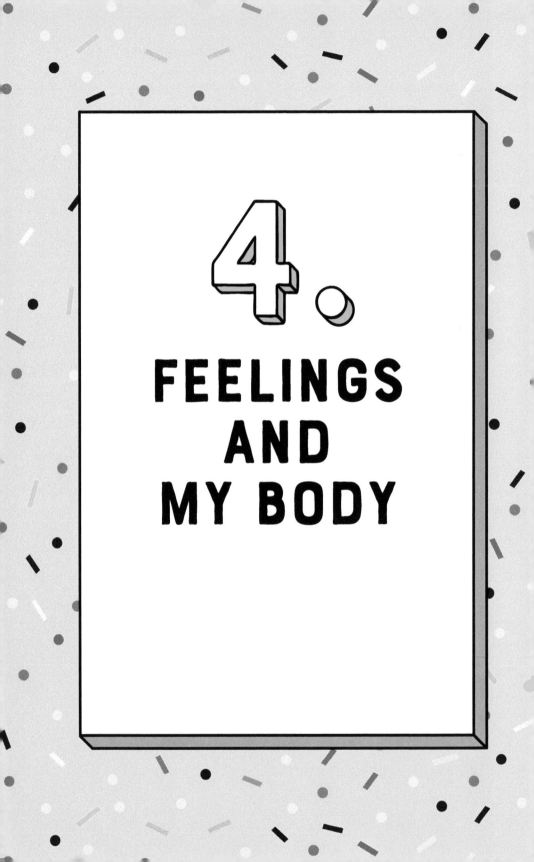

4.

FEELINGS AND MY BODY

Guess who's really happy right now? Emotional Eddie. That's because this whole chapter is all about him—he's the star! You see, Eddie plays a big part in how your body reacts to things. The emotional part of your brain tells the rest of your body what to do.

As you know, Eddie is always on alert for danger. When he senses trouble, he will tell you to put on your boxing gloves or your running shoes. Eddie is telling your body to either fight or take off and get out of there fast! He might even tell your body to just freeze. When these things happen, your heart may beat really fast and your muscles may get tight. You may even feel like you have to pee or poop! (Yes, I said poop.) These are just a few things you can feel when Eddie sends his signal to the nerves in your body. These responses are all completely natural, so let's explore how your feelings affect your body.

EXPRESS MYSELF

Did you know your body is always sending you messages? Just think about it. Your body tells you when you're hungry or thirsty, or hot or cold. And it tells you when you're feeling good or bad! Pay attention to these signals. They might be trying to tell you something so you can deal with it.

- If you can usually eat a lot, but you haven't wanted to eat much in a while, there may be something that you need to talk about.

- If you cry easily or more than usual, think about what's going on. Is there something troubling you?

ANTS IN MY PANTS AND BUTTERFLIES IN MY TUMMY

One time, when I had to sing in front of hundreds of people, I was very nervous. Emotional Eddie decided he needed to "rescue" me. He sent his signal to my body while I was singing. All of a sudden, my mouth

was so dry! His signal actually stopped my mouth from staying wet on the inside. I'm sure no one watching could tell a thing, but I could feel the inside of my top lip sticking to my teeth!

A dry mouth is just one way your body could react to your feelings. Let's talk about some more ways your body might react.

Ants in your pants: You just can't sit still! You need to keep moving because your nerves are super active. Your body gives you an extra burst of energy. This can happen when you are nervous or excited.

Butterflies: Butterflies are that fluttery feeling you get in your tummy when you feel nervous or excited. Your emotional brain stops your tummy from doing its usual job, which causes the feeling.

Blushing: This can happen when you feel embarrassed. If Eddie sends his signal, your face will turn red or feel hot for a minute or two.

Sweating: Eddie's signal may make you sweat all of a sudden. You may begin to sweat when you are afraid, nervous, worried, or even disgusted. Sweating is your body's way of cooling down.

Shaking: Your hands or body may shake when you are afraid, nervous, or excited. Eddie's signal will send extra energy to parts of your body, which causes you to shake.

Crying: You may cry when you are angry, afraid, embarrassed, or even really happy. This reaction happens when you don't hold your feelings inside.

Emotional Eddie is a pretty busy part of your brain. Have you ever had any of these reactions to your feelings? Can you remember when?

What's Happening in My Body?

Check out the list of reactions below. I'm sure you have felt some of these in your body before. See if you can match the situation on the left with a reaction on the right.

Situation	Possible Reactions
You drop your pencil on the floor. When you reach to pick it up, you see that it rolled next to a large spider.	Ants in Your Pants
Right in the middle of the school play, you forget your lines.	Blushing
You get in trouble at school. Your mom says no screen time for the next week.	Butterflies in Your Tummy
There's a surprise party for your sister today, and you're waiting for her to arrive.	Shaking
The principal has asked to see you in his office, but you aren't sure why. You're about to walk in . . .	Crying
The teacher tells you to stop talking and your classmates are looking at you.	Sweating

WHAT TO DO WHEN I FEEL . . .

There are things you can do when your body reacts to your emotions and feelings. Before we talk about those things, let's find out what your natural reaction would be!

Imagine you are in the following situation:

Your teacher has asked you to be a buddy to a new student. Your job is to explain how things work in the classroom. You also need to introduce him to three new friends. You are excited that your teacher chose you, but you begin to feel nervous once you meet him. As you talk to him, you notice your hands are beginning to shake. What should you do?

Choose the answer that best describes how you would respond.

a. Try to make the feeling go away. Concentrate really hard until your hands stop shaking.

b. Focus on your breathing. Take slow, deep breaths in between each thing you say.

c. Think about what might happen if you don't do the job your teacher asked you to do.

d. Try to do everything like your classmate did the last time she showed a new student around.

The best answer is **b**. Now, let's find out why!

The best first step is to think about your breathing. When your hands are shaking or you feel butterflies in your tummy, deep breathing will help you calm down. It's always best to breathe in through your nose. Breathe out through your mouth, and let that breath go a little longer. When you do this, your body will tell Eddie that the danger isn't going to hurt you. Also, remind yourself that the feeling you are having is temporary. Now let's discuss why the other choices in the quiz weren't the best choices.

Answer a: *Try to make the feeling go away. Concentrate really hard until your hands stop shaking.*

Don't try this because thinking about your hands shaking will only make the problem worse. Instead, focus on what you need to get done.

Answer c: *Think about what might happen if you don't do the job your teacher asked you to do.*

Don't think about what will happen if you mess up. This will make you more nervous, and you might even forget what you need to say or do. Stay focused on what you are doing.

Answer d: *Try to do everything like your classmate did the last time she showed a new student around.*

Don't think about what someone else did. You do YOU the best. Don't compare yourself to others. When it's over, you might decide that you want to do something differently next time, and that's okay. But you might not. You might decide that you did something even better than the person who had the job before you!

LOVE MYSELF

When your body reacts to emotions:

* Remind yourself that you are brave and capable of doing the thing that makes you so nervous.
* Tell yourself that you are doing your best, and everyone reacts to their emotions sometimes.
* When your nerves get the best of you, it doesn't mean there is anything wrong with you. Keep practicing!

FINDING MY BRAVE SELF

Our mind and body really go through a lot, don't they? We all experience so many different emotions and reactions every single day. But even with the butterflies in your belly and your shaking hands, there is a part of you that is brave! You do things all the time that take you out of your comfort zone. Think about it—every time you go out on the playground, or join a new club, or meet new people, you're doing something new and exciting!

In this chapter, you've gotten to know:

* Emotional Eddie causes your body to react the way it does when he needs to keep you safe.

* Your body reacts differently in different situations.

* There are things you can do to take control of your reactions.

* We all overreact sometimes, and it's okay!

From now on, when you experience different emotions, the smart and brave you will understand the feelings you have in your body a whole lot better than you did before. And you'll know just what to do! Just keep learning and growing, and you'll be the boss of Eddie in no time. All you can ever do is your best.

So, how do all of these emotions and feelings connect to your life? Let's find out!

5.

FEELINGS
AND
MY LIFE

Think of your life as a puzzle. There are a lot of pieces, right? One piece of your puzzle is the people who are important to you, like your family and friends. Another piece is school and all that goes on there each day. And, let's not forget your hobbies and activities—all the things you like to do in your free time.

In this chapter, we will talk about your feelings and how they affect your relationships, your time at school, and the things you like to do every day. We'll also talk about why it's important to understand how others are feeling, too. Are you ready? Let's put your puzzle together!

My Relationship Skills

Let's test your relationship skills! What would you do in each situation?

1. Your friend isn't talking much. You're not sure what's wrong. You:

   a. don't say anything. She gets like that sometimes.

   b. wait to see if she says anything so you know it's safe to talk about it.

   c. ask if something is bothering her and see if she wants to talk about it.

2. Your mom told you to clean your room, but you still haven't. She's in your doorway looking at you, and she's not smiling. You:

   a. yell that your brother's room isn't clean either, and that it's not fair.

   b. give an excuse about why it's not done and promise to start soon.

   c. jump up, apologize, and get to work cleaning your room.

3. A classmate upsets you at school, and your teacher notices and asks you to come talk with her about it. You:

   a. say, "I don't want to talk to anybody!"

b. say, "Not now, thanks. Maybe another day."

c. accept the teacher's offer to talk in private.

4. Your basketball coach says you've got to focus more and stop joking around at practice to stay on the team. You:

a. don't think she's right, and keep doing what you've always done.

b. try to focus and pay attention more, but there's still room for a joke or two.

c. tell the coach you're sorry and focus on being a good teammate and player.

Give yourself 1 point for every a, 2 points for every b, and 3 points for every c.

What's your score? _____

If your score was 4–5: Your relationships will really benefit from this chapter! Remember that you aren't the only person experiencing feelings; other people are as well.

If your score was 6–10: You have some good skills with some room to grow. Just keep working at it!

If your score was 11–12: Your relationship skills are strong—way to go!

MY FEELINGS AND FRIENDSHIPS

Good friends are people you care about and who care about you. When it comes to your feelings, it helps to have good friends. When good things happen for you, your friends will celebrate with you. And when things aren't so great, your friends will be there to help. When you have a good friend you trust, you can talk with that person about your feelings and they'll help you to work through them—and hopefully you can help them, too!

As a school counselor, I talk a lot about friendship with kids. Friendship problems are so common that probably everyone you've ever met in your life has had a problem with a friend at one time or another. That includes your parents, your teachers, and even your principal! Take a look at the friendship problem below. Does it sound familiar?

Sydney and Avery are good friends. This year, Hayden is in their class. Avery and Hayden have become friends, too. But Sydney feels jealous when Avery plays with Hayden. She starts to feel left out. Avery isn't trying to leave Sydney out; she's just play-ing with another friend. Sydney won't play with them because she just wants it to be her and Avery.

Has this ever happened to you? Sometimes you may feel angry, jealous, or sad because of things that happen in your friendships. It's important to be honest with your friends about your feelings so you can work things out. It's also important to try and understand how your friends feel, too. A true friend will want to make things better—can you both be a good friend and compromise? Sydney could try to accept and understand that Avery has another friend, and Avery can make sure to invite Sydney over after school so they can play alone. That will make everyone happy in the end!

EXPRESS MYSELF

When you need to share something difficult with a friend:

- **Be specific. Tell your friend what is bothering you and how it makes you feel. Your friend can't read your mind!**

- **Think about how the problem can be fixed and share your idea with your friend.**

- **Try to listen to your friend's side of the story and ask yourself, "What am I learning? Can I do something to make this better?"**

MY FEELINGS AND FAMILY

The people in your family are the closest people to you. Even so, there are still times you may have negative feelings about them. If you have brothers or sisters, you probably know what I mean! Maybe one of your siblings ate something you saved to eat later. Maybe you feel treated unfairly. You might have a baby brother or sister who gets lots of extra attention. This may make you feel jealous or forgotten. There may also be times when you don't agree with your mom or dad.

This can be really hard because your parents are in charge, and you may feel like there is nothing you can do about it. Guess what? It's still important to do something about your feelings. No matter what the problem may be, you should always talk about what you are feeling. Talking about your feelings will help you feel better, and hopefully it will start you on your way to getting your problem solved.

I've talked to many kids who never really think about telling their parents how they feel about things. As a parent myself, believe me: Your parents care about how you are feeling! They want the best for you, so don't be afraid to speak up and calmly ask if you can talk to them, then let them know what's going on inside you. You may be very surprised at how they respond!

Seven Steps to Calm

What can you do when you're with your family and your emotions get high? When you need to calm down and find some peace, here's something you can try:

1. Find a place to sit. Close your eyes and focus on your breathing.

2. Breathe in through your nose for a count of three.

3. Breathe out through your mouth for a count of five.

4. Take your strong emotions and pretend to squeeze them tight in your hands. Squeeze as tight as you can for five to seven seconds. Then open your hands and let them go. Notice how relaxed your hands feel when you release them.

5. Repeat, but this time add your toes. Squeeze for five to seven seconds, and let go.

6. Repeat one more time, but this time squeeze your entire body. Squeeze for five to seven seconds, and let go.

7. As you relax, continue to focus on your breathing. Open your eyes when you are ready.

How do you feel now? Hopefully you are more relaxed and ready to talk about your feelings or move on with your day!

MY FEELINGS AND SCHOOL

Did you know you spend about 35 hours a week at school? That's a lot of time! It's no surprise that you may go through tons of different feelings daily.

As a person who works in a school, I know there is much more to being at school than just learning. You're also trying to make friends and figure out where you fit in. It's not easy. You may feel lonely or sad. If there are kids who are not so nice, you might feel afraid or angry. You might also feel worried if your schoolwork is too hard, or bored if it's too easy. On top of that, you still have to learn and do well! The way you feel each day affects your ability to do that.

It's important to keep your cool at school and keep Eddie under control. Remember the exercises and tips you've learned in this book, and try some of them out at school when Eddie starts to come out, such as 5-4-3-2-1 (page 66) and Seven Steps to Calm (page 88).

If you don't feel so great about school for whatever reason, talk with a teacher about what's going on. They can help you figure out ways to make things better. Also, your school counselor is always on hand to talk with you about your feelings. Together, you can come up with things you can do to feel better and make your time at school easier. Then your brain will be ready for all the important things you need to learn!

LOVE MYSELF

If you're facing a challenge at school, try to:

* Talk to the people at school who are there to help you. You are not in this alone.

* Remember that taking care of your feelings will help you do your best in school. Your schoolwork is important, but so are you!

* Tell a trusted grown-up at home what's going on so they can help you, too.

MY FEELINGS AND HOBBIES

Earlier in the book, I told you that I was a cheerleader in school. It was just one of the things I liked to do as a kid. You may also cheer or play a sport. You might make crafts, dance, or play an instrument. These are all great hobbies. Having a hobby is especially cool because you can be around other people who also like the same thing. This means you can meet more friends who have things in common with you.

These extra activities are meant to make you feel happy. But sometimes there are negative feelings that may come up, too. You may feel worried that you won't make the team or get the position you want to play. You might compare yourself with others and feel like you're not as good as you want to be.

When I was a kid, I played the clarinet. I was pretty good at it, too. I would practice a lot at home. I was first chair (which is an honor to get), and I wanted to stay there. Oh, the pressure! When you're good at something, and you get recognized for your talent, that's a great feeling. But it can also come with a not-so-good feeling: the pressure of staying on top.

It's important to remind yourself that you enjoy the thing you're doing, no matter what position you end up with. The time you spend doing your hobby can be a great way to make your life more enjoyable, and it can also take your mind off any negative feelings from other parts of your life. Look at that— another strategy!

PUTTING MYSELF IN THEIR SHOES

I want to tell you about an important word. It's called empathy. Empathy is when you imagine how you would feel in another person's position. Have you ever heard of "putting yourself in another person's shoes"? It's not always easy, but learning how to do this will help you understand others a lot better. Remember, others want their feelings to be heard, just like you do. After all, how would you feel if someone didn't respect your feelings?

Think about it this way: What if something happened with a friend that made you very upset? And when you told your friend you were upset, they simply said to you, "Get over it!" That wouldn't feel good, would it?

It would feel a lot better if, instead of telling you to "get over it," your friend said, "I can understand why this would make you feel upset." If they said that, you would know that your friend really understands and respects how you feel. It doesn't mean that they agree with you completely—it just means that they are trying to see the situation from your side.

The lesson here is this: If you and a friend are angry with each other, don't just think about how you feel; think about how your friend feels, too. Try to understand their point of view. In the end, it can make you a better friend and a better person. In fact, it's a skill that will help you get along with others through your entire life!

I'M IN CHARGE!

In this chapter, we explored all kinds of ways we can use our emotions and feelings to make our lives better—whether it's in our relationships with family and friends, our time at school, or our favorite activities. You've learned:

- There are ways to communicate better in relationships.

- You can be a better friend by using compromise and empathy.

- It is important to share your feelings with family and friends.

- There are people at school and home who can help you with your feelings.

- Hobbies are a great way to make friends and feel good about yourself.

Now on to chapter 6 to learn some easy tips for dealing with different emotions!

6.

WHAT TO DO WHEN . . .

Dealing with tough emotions and feelings can be hard. Sometimes you just may not know what to do. But I've got you covered. This last chapter is full of tips you can check out whenever you need them.

The chapter covers three main negative emotions: sadness, anger, and anxiety. Although these tips are grouped by sad, angry, and anxious feelings, many of them can be used for all three feelings. You can also use many of these tips for when you're feeling other feelings too, like jealousy or fear. I hope these tips come in handy for you in all kinds of situations.

TIPS FOR WHEN I FEEL SAD

1. **Talk with someone you trust.** Talking things through can help you feel so much better. You may also get advice that can really help you.

2. **Stay active doing something.** Exercising is good for our emotions as well as our body. You might enjoy jumping rope or riding your bike. Whatever your favorite exercise is, get out there and do it!

3. **Play or cuddle with a pet.** Pets have a way of making you feel calm, and they're always happy to see you. A good cuddle with my dog always helps me.

4. **Look for the bright side.** For example, if you and your best friend don't get placed in the same class, try to think of it as a chance for both of you to make new friends.

5. **Write about your feelings.** It can help to write about what you are feeling and why. You can share it with someone you trust or keep it to yourself.

6. **Play with a good friend.** This will help take your mind away from your sad feelings. If you can't get together, call or text them.

7. **Keep your routine.** Routines offer calmness and comfort. When times get tough, do what you usually do each day, as though nothing is different.

8. **Do something that makes you happy.** If it's coloring, color. If it's playing video games, game on. Whatever it is, do it for yourself.

9. **Do something kind for someone else.** Making another person (or even a pet) happy will make you feel good, too!

10. **Allow yourself to feel sad.** Let your feelings go. Cry and let it all out. Remember, crying can help you feel better. We all need a good cry every now and then!

TIPS FOR WHEN I FEEL ANGRY

1. Know your triggers! You can't control everything that makes you angry, but some things you can. When you learn the things that make you angry, you will be ready if they happen and can react in the best way.

2. Pay attention to where you feel anger in your body. Emotional Eddie might cause your heart to beat faster or your fists to tighten. If you notice anger in your body, try to get away from the situation so things don't get worse.

3. Count backward from any number. Just pick one: 49 . . . 10 . . . 87! When you count backward, your brain will focus on the numbers instead of the thing that made you feel angry.

4. Decide how angry you are on a scale from 1 to 10. Ten would be REALLY angry and 1 would be barely angry at all. Plan for what you will do if you are an 8, 9, or 10. While you're at it, why not make a plan for all the numbers?

5. Turn your angry energy into something positive. Use your energy to clean your room, run, or play a game.

6. Share how you are feeling. Let people know if they are making you angry. Say, "I feel angry because _____."

7. Think before you act. Use "if-then" statements. ("*If* I do this, *then* this will happen.") If your "then" is going to hurt someone or get you into trouble, make a different choice!

8. Find a chill-out spot. Have a place where you can go to get your mind off things. You can even ask your teacher to help you create one in your classroom.

9. Get help from an adult or friend. The people who care about you are there to help you talk through your problems. Use them!

10. Take deep breaths. Remember to breathe in through your nose, and then out through your mouth for a few seconds longer—this will calm your body (see page 88).

TIPS FOR WHEN I FEEL ANXIOUS

1. Always check your thoughts. Are your thoughts telling the truth? Remember that your thoughts will sometimes tell you things that are not really true. Use your thinking brain to decide what's real.

2. Find something to do with your hands. Fidget toys are great. You can even make your own by slicing a pool noodle into smaller pieces. They're strong enough to squeeze and keep your hands busy. You can also put beads on a safety pin. And let's not forget that faithful stress ball or fidget spinner!

3. Do something relaxing. If you're anxious, find a way to relax your body and mind: maybe floating around in the pool, painting, reading, or just lying in the grass and looking up at the clouds.

4. Stay in the now. No time traveling allowed! When you feel nervous or anxious about something that is happening soon, try to stay in the present moment. Thinking about that future event may make the reactions in your body worse. Try not to put pictures of the worst outcome in your head. Instead, picture the best possible outcome!

5. Avoid "avoiding things"! Anxiety usually happens when you feel nervous about something. When you are nervous, you may avoid the things that worry you—but this can make things worse and make you feel less confident. Instead of avoiding those things, take a "can-do" attitude and tackle them head on!

6. Control your breathing. Blowing bubbles is great for calming anxiety. They help you breathe in and then breathe out a little longer. You can pretend there's a flower on the end of a pinwheel. Smell the flower, then blow the pinwheel.

7. Find something to distract you. When I'm singing and feeling nervous, I focus on something in the back of the room or a smiling face. It really helps!

8. Send your brain on a scavenger hunt! Find all the green things in the room. Find all the things that are blue as you walk down the hallway.

9. Get a hug from someone who loves you. Or give one to yourself!

10. Strike a power pose! Look at yourself in the mirror and stand like a superhero or a brave warrior. Throw your shoulders back, put your hands on your waist, and stand tall. You've got the power!

Always remember that all of your feelings are natural. It's okay to feel them. It can take a while to figure out how to get control over your emotions. There are many adults out there in the world who are still trying! So don't give up if it doesn't happen quickly enough. Just keep reading this book and practicing the exercises that work for you. You have what it takes to handle what comes your way—you know what to do. I just wish I could be there to see your face when you take charge of your feelings—you're going to feel great!

RESOURCES

It's fun to read picture books about kids who may be going through the same things you are or to read books that have great ideas for dealing with your feelings. Here are a few to check out:

- Cain, Janan. *The Way I Feel*. New York, NY: Scholastic Inc., 2001.

- Cook, Julia, and Allison Valentine. *Soda Pop Head*. Chattanooga, TN: National Center for Youth Issues, 2011.

- Curtis, Jamie Lee, and Laura Cornell. *Today I Feel Silly & Other Moods That Make My Day*. New York, NY: Harper Collins, 1998.

- Garcia, Gabi, and Ying Hui Tan. *Listening to My Body*. Austin, Texas: Skinned Knee Publishing, 2017.

- Sornson, Bob, and Shelley Johannes. *Stand in My Shoes: Kids Learning About Empathy*. Golden, CO: Love and Logic Press, 2013.

- Verde, Susan, and Peter H. Reynolds. *I Am Human: A Book of Empathy*. New York, NY: Abrams Books, 2018.

- Verdick, Elizabeth, and Ray Cruz, and Marjorie Lisovskis. *How to Take the Grrrr Out of Anger*. Minneapolis, MN: Free Spirit Publishing, 2015.

- Viorst, Judith, and Ray Cruz. *Alexander and the Terrible, Horrible, No Good, Very Bad Day*. New York, NY: Atheneum Books for Young Readers, 1987.

You can also check out these websites just for kids:

- www.kidshealth.org/en/kids/feeling — Choose a link and find lots of helpful tips about emotions and behaviors.

- www.cyh.com — Click on Kid's Health and then (under Topics) click Your Feelings. Here you will see many links for topics like worrying about things, being happy, feeling lonely, and stress.

Be sure to have permission from a parent before visiting any websites.

ACKNOWLEDGMENTS

To Orli—Thank you for your guidance throughout this process and for being my Thinking Thelma when Emotional Eddie ruffled my feathers!

To Patty—Thanks so much for helping me fine-tune everything. You are great at what you do!

To Anna, Valerie, and LaVerne—Thanks for answering those spur-of-the-moment questions as I was thinking through my writing.

To Aubrey—Your help was MAGICAL! (Wink.) Thank you so much!

ABOUT THE AUTHOR

 **Vanessa Green Allen, MEd, NBCT** is a professional school counselor living in Raleigh, North Carolina. She is the author of *The No More Bullying Book for Kids*. She received her bachelor of arts degree in elementary education from North Carolina Central University and her master of education degree in counseling from North Carolina State University. Vanessa is a former second-grade teacher, and she has worked for the Wake County Public School System since 1991. She is a 2009 National Board–certified teacher in the area of school counseling. Vanessa is also the creator and author of SavvySchoolCounselor.com, where she shares ideas and resources with school counselors across the globe.

CPSIA information can be obtained
at www.ICGtesting.com
Printed in the USA
BVHW091649100520
579362BV00010B/100